Always
& Forever

FRIENDSHIP ACTIVITIES FOR YOU AND ME

**This book is dedicated to my parents,
who are unfailingly dedicated to me.**

Special thanks to Ms. Jessica Lonski's class
(especially Jennifer Martin) in Niagara Falls, New York.

ISBN 0-439-68692-X

12 11 10 9 8 7 6   6 7 8 9/0
Printed in the U.S.A.
First printing, October 2004

BOOK DESIGN BY JENNIFER RINALDI WINDAU

Perfect World

Always & Forever

FRIENDSHIP ACTIVITIES FOR YOU AND ME

By **Rosanne Colosi**
Illustrated by **Angela Martini**

Scholastic Inc.

New York   Toronto   London   Auckland   Sydney
Mexico City   New Delhi   Hong Kong   Buenos Aires

What's Hot Inside

INTRODUCTION

Have you ever heard someone say,

"THOSE TWO ARE JOINED AT THE HIP"?

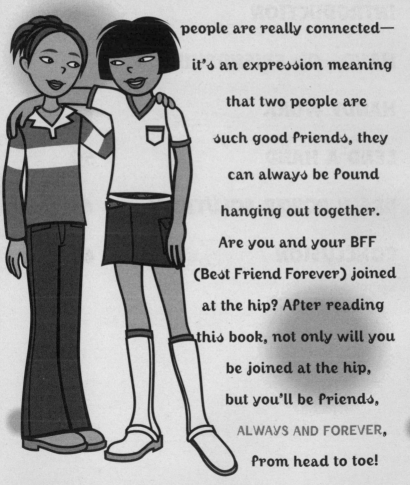

Of course, it doesn't mean that two people are really connected— it's an expression meaning that two people are such good friends, they can always be found hanging out together. Are you and your BFF (Best Friend Forever) joined at the hip? After reading this book, not only will you be joined at the hip, but you'll be friends, ALWAYS AND FOREVER, from head to toe!

HANDS-ON FRIENDSHIP

DIY BEAUTY

Lip-Smacking Lip Gloss

INGREDIENTS:

Clean and empty film canister or other small
    plastic container

Petroleum jelly

Cocoa powder (or powdered juice mix in cherry,
    lemonade, or another favorite flavor)

Put several teaspoons of petroleum jelly
(enough to almost fill the film canister) in a
microwave-safe dish. With an adult's help, place
it in the microwave for 15 seconds, then remove
and stir. Continue stirring until the petroleum
jelly has melted.

Add half a teaspoon of cocoa powder or powdered juice mix, then stir, and microwave the
mixture for another 30 seconds. (You can add
more if you would like a stronger flavor.)

When the mixture cools down a little, transfer
it to the film canister and let it cool completely.
Then smooth it onto your lips with your finger-
tips, grab a mirror, and smile at the result of
your work!

Groovy Grapefruit Mask

INGREDIENTS:

1 teaspoon of grapefruit juice

1 teaspoon of sour cream

1 egg white

Use a fork or a whisk to beat the egg white until it is completely fluffy. Add the sour cream and grapefruit juice and mix everything together. Apply gently to your face, leave on for about 15 minutes, and then rinse off. This mask works well for oily skin...and for scaring your little brother!

Orange Yogurt Mask

Take a quarter of an **orange** and squeeze the juice into a bowl. Add a teaspoon of **plain yogurt** and mix well. Apply to your face, leave on for 5 minutes, and rinse off. This mask will leave you feeling fresh and energized—absolutely perfect to charge you up for a busy week!

Apple-a-Day Conditioner

INGREDIENTS:

1 large apple, peeled and divided into small pieces

2 tablespoons of apple cider vinegar

2 cups of water

With an adult's help, put all of the ingredients into a food processor or blender and mix at the highest speed. When it looks as if the ingredients have blended together, pour through a strainer, getting rid of all the apple chunks that may be left.

First shampoo and rinse, then pour the conditioner over your hair, massaging it through, just as you would with shampoo. Rinse the conditioner from your hair with cool water. Your hair will be shiny for days!

Honey, Don't You Look Good! Lotion

Put 1 teaspoon of **honey**, 1 teaspoon of **vegetable oil**, and a quarter teaspoon of **lemon juice** in a bowl and stir. That's all you have to do to start yourself on your way to smoother skin!

You can put this mixture on your elbows, hands, legs—anywhere your skin needs moisturizing. Leave it on for 10 minutes, then rinse it off with cool water.

Swirly-Girly Body Glitter

INGREDIENTS: *(all can be purchased at the supermarket)*

Aloe vera gel

Food coloring

Glitter

Clean and empty film canister (or other sealable small container)

Pour the aloe vera gel into the container until it is about three-fourths full. Add two drops of food coloring and stir. Continue to add food coloring, one drop at a time and stirring after each drop, until you reach a color that you love. Adding more food coloring will make the color darker. Stir in the glitter a little at a time to avoid clumping.

You can use as much food coloring and glitter as you like. For a fun look, try adding little confetti cutouts in the theme of your choice.

Use on your arms, legs, or cheeks, but be sure to avoid your eyes. The glitter washes off with soap and water.

Don't forget to show off your new look!

INCREDIBLE EDIBLES

A favorite summer activity is strawberry picking. Instead of buying strawberries at the supermarket, grab a hat, sunscreen, and your best friend, and head out to the strawberry fields to pick them yourself. It will make your strawberry dishes taste that much sweeter!

Berry Cute Little Cakes

Here's a quick recipe. Isn't it fun to make something delicious in just a few minutes?

INGREDIENTS:

2 pints of strawberries (approx.)

Individual sponge cakes (can be bought
    ready-made at the supermarket—they
    look like empty cupcake wrappers)

1 cup of sugar

Whipped topping (store bought or homemade)

Fill each individual cake with strawberries. You should make sure they're full, but be careful that the strawberry mountain doesn't cause an avalanche! Sprinkle sugar on top, and dab a spoonful of whipped topping on each one.

The hardest part will be stopping yourself from eating them all at once!

Summer Strawberry Salad

INGREDIENTS:

1 head of romaine lettuce, torn into small pieces
1 cucumber, peeled and sliced
Strawberries, as many as you like!

This is another easy dish. Just combine all of the ingredients in a large bowl. Use two wooden spoons to mix the ingredients evenly. If you're feeling creative, add other fruits or toppings to the salad.

Turn the page for the delicious salad dressing!

SALAD DRESSING INGREDIENTS:

4 tablespoons of liquid honey

4 tablespoons of salad oil

3 tablespoons of balsamic vinegar

1 teaspoon poppy seeds (optional)

Place all four ingredients into a container with a lid. Make sure the lid is tightly sealed, and shake away. Pour over the salad and serve.

TASTY TIP—Strawberries are delicious all year round, not just in the summer. So if you want to bring a little sunshine into a cold winter day, just use frozen strawberries!

Who doesn't love a good marshmallow? They're one of the most fun and tasty treats around, especially if you have a sweet tooth. So have fun with these marshmallow-y good recipes!

Fruity Delight

INGREDIENTS:

1 can of pineapple tidbits (well drained)

1 small can of mandarin oranges (well drained)

2 cups of whipped topping

1/2 cup of coconut flakes

1 cup of small, colored marshmallows

1/4 cup of chopped maraschino cherries

3 tablespoons of milk

Well, there's bad news and good news, folks.

The bad news is that this recipe has a lot of different ingredients.

The good news is that it's super easy to make!

Thoroughly mix up all the ingredients and refrigerate for one hour.

Then grab a spoon and dig in!

Marshmallow Makeover

Marshmallows all look pretty similar, right? They're round, puffy, pillowy things. And they have been for years.

Isn't it time to give marshmallows a makeover?

All you need is a package of large marshmallows, a rolling pin, and a small cookie cutter. Take one of the large marshmallows and use the rolling pin to roll it as flat as possible. Then use the cookie cutter to cut out a shape, just as you would with cookie dough. Voilá! You have a fun marshmallow shape to put in your hot chocolate!

Hot Fudge Sundae Pie

Okay, ladies. . .this is a tough recipe, but if you have conquered the other recipes in this book, I'll bet you can make this pie with flying colors! Plus, it's so delicious that it's worth the trouble!

CHOCOLATE CRUMB CRUST INGREDIENTS:

1-1/4 cup of finely chopped chocolate
   cookie wafers

1/4 cup of chopped nuts (almonds, walnuts, etc.)

3 tablespoons of sugar

6 tablespoons of melted butter or margarine

To make the crust, combine the cookie crumbs, nuts, and sugar in a bowl and mix well. Then pour the melted butter or margarine over the mixture and toss lightly until everything is well blended. Press mixture into the bottom and up the sides of a 9-inch or 10-inch pie plate. Cover it with plastic wrap and put it in the fridge for 30 minutes.

Please turn the page for the rest of the recipe.

FILLING INGREDIENTS

1 quart of softened vanilla ice cream

1 quart of softened chocolate ice cream

1/2 cup of whipped topping
(store bought or made)

1 jar of hot fudge sauce, heated according to
directions on jar (or you can use chocolate
syrup instead)

To make the filling, spread half of the softened vanilla ice cream evenly over the crust and put the pie in the freezer until the ice cream has refrozen. Take it out of the freezer and drizzle half of the hot fudge over the top. The fudge will become solid because the ice cream is so cold. Spread the remaining vanilla ice cream over the fudge. Return the pie to the freezer until it is firm.

TOPPING INGREDIENTS

Coarsely chopped walnuts

Maraschino cherries, rinsed and drained

Ready for more ice cream? Scoop balls of chocolate ice cream on top of the layers of vanilla. Drizzle the remaining hot fudge over the top. Spoon the whipped cream on top. And decorate the pie with the nuts and cherries.

Cover the pie with plastic wrap and store it in the freezer. Just take it out of the freezer about 30 minutes before you're ready to eat it. Or invite 10 to 12 of your closest friends to your house and eat it right away!

Ribbon Mania!

Create new looks for just a few dollars! Sound impossible? Never! Many of the hottest looks right now involve ribbons, so why not make a ribbon belt to update your old skirt?

Ribbon belts are inexpensive and easy to make. Just go to your local crafts store and head for the ribbon aisle. The best kind of ribbon to use for a belt is 1-2 inches wide. To get an exact match, bring your skirt or pants and try to slide the ribbon through the belt loops.

When you find ribbon that you like, ask a salesperson to help measure the length you will need. You can generally make a belt with about one yard of ribbon. The salesperson will cut the ribbon for you.

At home, try on the skirt or pants and guide the ribbon through the belt loops. Instead of tying it in front (where your belt buckle is), tie it in a bow on your right hip. You can make the bow as big as you want and let the ends dangle as long as you want. Once you decide on a length, cut the ends of the ribbon on an angle, and you're ready to go out on the town!

Fashion Notes

Some ribbon frays easily, so you might need
to dip the ends in glue to seal them. Make sure
to ask the salesperson for details.

You can also look for a neat buckle
to make the belt extra special.

If you really want your ribbon to stand out,
make sure that the rest of your outfit consists
of whites, blacks, or khaki or jean material.
These plain colors will make the belt
the focus of your outfit.

Sometimes ribbon that looks wild and crazy
at the store will look the most chic on your outfit. When searching for the perfect pattern,
try holding it up against white or black fabric.

Ribbon can be used for a variety of other
accessories: chokers, bracelets, headbands, pins
...use your imagination!

HANDY WORK

GAMES GALORE

Brainpower

How well do you know your BFF? Sure, you probably know her birthday and her shoe size, but do you know her *really* well? Fill out one page and have your BFF fill out the other page. Then compare notes!

MY PAGE

My BFF's name is _____.

If my BFF had a million dollars, the first thing she'd do is

_____.

Her most drool-worthy celebrity crush is _____.

The CD most likely to be playing in her CD player is

_____.

In five years, my BFF will probably

_____.

The present she wants most for her birthday this year is

_____.

We are BFFs because _____

_____.

MY BFF'S PAGE

My BFF's name is _____.

If my BFF had a million dollars, the first thing she'd do is

_____.

Her most drool-worthy celebrity crush is _____.

The CD most likely to be playing in her CD player is

_____.

In five years, my BFF will probably

_____.

The present she wants most for her birthday this year is

_____.

We are BFFs because _____

_____.

WINDOW TELEPHONE

You've probably played the old game of Telephone, right? It's the one where everyone sits in a circle and whispers a sentence to the next person, so that a phrase that started out as "Cecilia loves to eat pizza" may turn into, "My sister does not know how to treat you."

In Window Telephone, the girl who is "It" goes outside and stands in front of a big window. The rest of the group gathers around the inside window so they can see It clearly. Then It whispers a sentence so that everyone inside can see her lips moving but can't hear what she's saying. Write your guesses down on pieces of paper and hold the papers up to the window so It can see them. Whoever guesses the sentence correctly becomes It for the next round.

If you think this is an easy game, try whispering "elephant shoes" to someone on the opposite side of a window. She will think you are saying "I love you."

TRY IT!

Say the following letters to your friend and ask her to pronounce them.

T-W-A

(She will respond, "Twaaah.")

T-W-E

(She will respond, "Tweee.")

T-W-I

(She will respond, "Twaaaiii.")

T-W-U

(She will respond, "Twuuu.")

T-W-O

(With any luck, she will respond, "Twooohhh." And then you can laugh with her for forgetting how to pronounce the word "two.")

YOUR TV RATINGS

We all know we should be outside getting fresh air...but every once in a while, it's relaxing to hang out with your friends, eat snacks, and watch some good television.

RATING SYSTEM

5—We have every episode on tape!

4—We watch this show every single week!

3—We'll watch it if we have nothing better to do.

2—Our annoying sisters might like it.

1—Ew! What show is that?!

How would you rate these television shows?

"Malcolm in the Middle" ———

"Friends" ———

"Even Stevens" ———

"That's So Raven" ———

"Seventh Heaven" ———

"Trading Spaces" ———

Now rank other shows!

TV Show   Rating

_____   _____

_____   _____

_____   _____

_____   _____

_____   _____

_____   _____

SURVIVOR BEE

What would you do if you were stranded on a desert island? What would you use to get rescued? This game will challenge you to come up with some answers...fast!

One person should be the Game Show Host. Give her three minutes to run around the room and grab any random small items she finds while everyone else waits outside the room. The Host places all of the items in front of her and covers them with a blanket.

Everyone reenters the room and stands next to one another in a straight line. One by one, each girl steps forward as the Host reveals an object from under the blanket. Then that girl has 10 seconds to figure out a way to use the object to survive on a desert island. The Host then decides whether the answer is acceptable.

For example, if the Host holds up a mirror, here is an acceptable answer:

"I would use the mirror to signal planes to rescue me."

Here is an unacceptable answer:

"I would use the mirror to see how I look in case Jeff from homeroom shows up on the island."

The rest of the game works just like a spelling bee. If the answer is acceptable to the Host, the girl stays in the game. If not, she is off the island! Continue playing until there is only one Survivor left!

SAMPLE ITEMS THAT CAN BE USED:

Sunglasses

Towel

Watch

Pencil

Umbrella

Shoelaces

Cup

Tights

CD

Masking tape

Lip gloss

Earrings

Bandanna

Scissors

Soda bottle

SUPER SECRET NOTES

Have you ever wanted to tell your friend a secret that you didn't want anyone else to hear? Instead of telling her, write it down!

If you are already an experienced secret note writer, you probably know that lemon juice makes terrific invisible ink. In case you're a new

secret note writer, here's what you do. Cut a lemon in half and squeeze the juice into a paper cup. Use a toothpick as a pencil by dipping it in the lemon juice "ink" before "writing" on paper. When the lemon juice dries, you can pass the note to a friend. She can hold it up in front of a lightbulb to make the writing magically appear.

Whether you're an amateur or a pro at invisible ink, you should know the most important part of secret note passing is having a decoy. A decoy is something used to mislead someone. In this case, your decoy will be a boring note. Use a regular pen to write a note about the weather, your lunch, or your homework.

Here comes the sneaky part: Write your secret letter between the lines of the decoy letter. This way, if anyone other than your BFF reads the letter, she will think it's only about the weather, lunch, or homework. Only your BFF will know to hold the letter up to the light to reveal the hidden message you have written just for her!

But remember, if you don't want your teacher to read your note out loud, don't pass notes in class!

Hi, Kristin!

Kristin—

Can you believe how much homework we have?!

We're voting for class president in homeroom today.

It will take me ALL NIGHT to finish!

Would you please nominate me?

Talk to you after school!

I think it would be fun to run!

Bye! Veronica

Later—V

Are you and your BFF in the mood to laugh? Check out these jokes!

● ● ● ● ● ● ● ● ● ● ● ● ● ●

YOU SAY TO YOUR FRIEND:
"Use your finger to point to your head."

(*Your friend points to her head.*)

YOU : **"Now, how do you abbreviate the word 'Mountain?'"**

YOUR FRIEND: **"MT."**

● ● ● ● ● ● ● ● ● ● ● ● ● ● ● ● ●

YOU SAY TO YOUR FRIEND:
"Use your finger to point to the sky."

(*Your friend points to the sky.*)

YOU: **"Now twirl your finger around and around in a circle and don't stop."**

(*Your friend twirls her finger in a circular motion.*)

YOU: **"Now I'm going to tell you a knock-knock joke. Knock, knock."**

YOUR FRIEND: **"Who's there?"** (*Still twirling.*)

YOU: **"Wah."**

YOUR FRIEND: **"Wah-who?"** (*Still twirling.*)

YOU: **"I didn't know you were going to throw yourself a party! Thanks for forgetting to invite me!"**

SUPER SLEUTH SHOWDOWN

Here's a great game to spice up any sleepover!
Cut out a square of paper for each girl playing,
and put an X on all of the squares except
for two. On one of the two leftover
squares, write D for "detective," and
on the other, write T for "thief."

T

Fold all the paper squares, put
them in a hat, and have each girl pick a square.
The girl who becomes the detective
leaves the room.

Turn off the lights and care-
fully move slowly around the
room. The girl who's the designat-
ed thief sneaks around the room and taps someone on the shoulder. The person who is tapped
should fall to the ground, saying, "Ahhhh!
Someone stole my purse!"

D

The detective rushes in to the scene
of the crime and looks around silently.
Then the detective announces her suspect. If she guesses incorrectly, she
plays the detective for another round. If
she guesses correctly, the thief becomes the
detective for the next round.

X

TONGUE TWISTERS!

Dare your BFF to say one of these
tongue twisters six times in a row!

**A skunk sat on a stump
and thunk the stump stunk,
but the stump thunk
the skunk stunk.**

One smart fellow, he felt smart.

Two smart fellows, they felt smart.

Three smart fellows, they all felt smart.

Unique New York.

MRS. SMITH'S
FISH SAUCE SHOP.

You've no need to light a night-light
On a light night like tonight,
For a night-light's light's a slight light,
And tonight's a night that's light.
When a night's light, like tonight's light,
It is really not quite right
To light night-lights with their slight lights
On a light night like tonight.

Sixish.

IF STU CHEWS SHOES,
SHOULD STU CHOOSE
THE SHOES HE CHEWS?

BE A MOVIE CRITIC!

Back when your grandparents and great-grand-parents were young, they probably used the expression "the bee's knees" to describe anything that was especially cool. If we still used that phrase today, we might say things like, "Have you heard that new CD? It's totally the bee's knees!" Crazy, right? Well here's a chance for you and your BFF to describe what's hot and what's not at the movie theater!

Rating System

5 —We loved it so much that we bought the DVD!

4 —It was so good that we forgot to

eat our popcorn!

3 —We would go see it if our parents paid

for the tickets.

2 —What were we thinking when we chose

to see that movie?

1 —We demand a refund!

Clueless

RATING: _____

The Cinderella Story

RATING: _____

Confessions of a Teenage Drama Queen

RATING: _____

Spider-Man 2

RATING: _____

Shrek 2

RATING: _____

Finding Nemo

RATING: _____

Now fill in and rate your own faves!

Movie   RATING

_____   _____

_____   _____

_____   _____

_____   _____

PROBLEM-SOLVING CHALLENGE

With all the tests you take at school, you've probably never taken a test like this one. It tests your use of logic and creativity. Play with your friends and see who can rise to the challenge! *(Answers appear on page 63.)*

1. A plane took off from Washington, D.C., and flew across the Atlantic Ocean to Paris, France. Unfortunately, the plane's engine failed and it fell into the ocean, exactly halfway between North America and Europe. There were both Americans and Europeans on the flight. Where were the survivors buried?

2. Put a dot on this letter:

I

3. You are driving a bus. At the first stop, 5 passengers get on. At the second stop, 20 passengers get on and 3 get off. At the third stop,

1 passenger gets on and 13 get off. At the fourth stop, 8 passengers get on and 5 get off. And at the last stop, 11 passengers get on and 19 passengers get off. What color are the bus driver's eyes?

4. A father and his son, Jason, were in a minor car accident. The father was rushed into one room in the hospital and the boy was rushed into another. A doctor thought Jason might need an operation on his broken wrist and brought in a surgeon. The surgeon shouted, "I can't operate on him. He's my son!" How can this be?

BIRTHDAY PRESENT SCAVENGER HUNT

Here's a great way to spice up your BFF's birthday party. Instead of just giving her presents, why not make her earn them?

Before you get to your BFF's party, let her parents and your friends in on your idea. While her parents keep her busy, you and your friends can hide the presents you brought. Then tell your BFF that in order to find her presents, she will have to tell some jokes!

She should tell one of her guests a joke. If the guest thinks the birthday girl's joke is satisfactory, she should give her a hint to find a present. If the guest doesn't like the joke, she can ask for another. But no one should reveal a present's location until after the joke is told. The birthday girl must continue telling jokes to each guest until she finds every present. You can be nice and give your BFF a joke book, or you can force her to remember or make up jokes by herself.

Here are some jokes to get you started:

What does a skeleton say when he wants to eat?
Bone appetit!

**I have a green nose, three red mouths, and four purple ears.
What am I?**
Ugly!

What do spiders like to order at a fast food restaurant?
Burgers and flies

First Student: "I'm taking French, Spanish, and Algebra this year."
*Second Student: "Okay. Let me hear you say
good evening in Algebra."*

What nails do carpenters hate to hit?
Fingernails

What do you call a very popular perfume?
A best-smeller

What goes "Oh, Oh, Oh?"
Santa walking backward

What is at the end of everything?
The letter G

**Why did the dolphin
cross the beach?**
To get to the other tide

What goes "tick, tick, woof, woof"?
A watchdog

WBFF FM

Do you sing in the shower? Do you and your BFF sing along with the car radio? Do you like to listen to your favorite songs over and over and over again? If you are a music lover, you will have no problem with this rating activity.

RATING SYSTEM

5 – We'll cry if they don't win a Grammy award!

4 – We have all the lyrics memorized!

3 – We'll listen to that CD if we're in the right mood.

2 – Anyone have some earplugs we can borrow?!

1 – Who is that?

How would you rate these musicians?

Britney Spears _____

Beyoncé _____

Blink-182 _____

Justin Timberlake _____

Hilary Duff _____

Outkast _____

How do other musicians stack up?

MUSICIAN/GROUP   RATING

_____   _____

_____   _____

_____   _____

_____   _____

_____   _____

_____   _____

WORD TEASERS

These word puzzles will test the creativity and problem-solving skills of you and your BFF. Try to decode each box! (*Answers are on page 63.*)

EXAMPLE:

FRIJUSTENDS

Just Between Friends

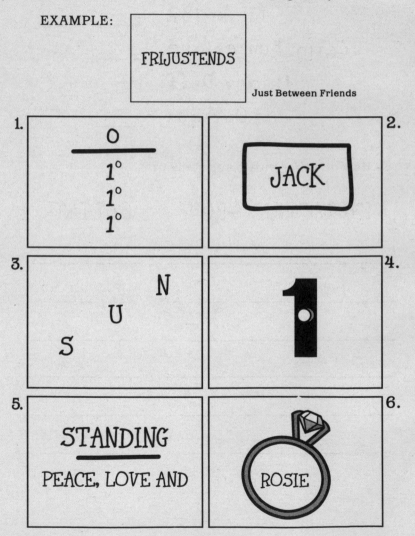

1.
$$\frac{O}{1^\circ}$$
1°
1°

2. JACK

3.
N
U
S

4. 1

5. STANDING
_____
PEACE, LOVE AND

6. ROSIE

THE MYSTERY OF THE MISSING DOLLAR

Three women enter a hotel, and they each pay $10 to rent a hotel room with three beds, which costs $30. They give the money to the clerk at the front desk, and they take their luggage to room 613.

Later, the clerk realizes that he overcharged them. The room should have cost only $25. The clerk, being the nice guy that he is, gives the bellboy five $1 bills to give back to the women. The bellboy brings the money to room 613. The women, being the nice women that they are, each take $1 and let the bellboy keep the extra $2.

Each woman originally paid $10, and they each accepted $1 from the bellboy. That means that each woman actually paid only $9. If three women paid $9 each, that means that together they paid $27 for the room. If the bellboy kept $2, that makes the total $29. But the women originally paid $30 total.

$9 x 3 = $27 $27 + $2 = $29

What happened to the missing dollar? (*Answer is on page 63.*)

SECRET MAILBOX

So maybe you don't feel like going to the trouble of using lemon juice to make invisible ink. Or maybe you just ran out of lemons. There are still many other ways that you can pass secret messages to your friends.

One way to pass secret messages is to make a secret mailbox. Of course, because this is a secret mailbox, it won't look anything like a real mailbox. In fact, it may not even be a mailbox at all. A secret mailbox is simply a drop-off area for you and your friends to leave notes.

The easiest way to do this is to use your family mailbox. Instead of putting your note inside the mailbox, tape it to the outside of the mailbox, either underneath or on the back. Your family will never suspect, but you and your BFF will know right where to look!

If you don't have a free-standing mailbox, you may choose an out-of-the-way outdoor location for your secret drop-off. You could place your note under a big rock next to a certain tree, leave it inside your tire swing, or put it inside the leaves of a bushy potted plant. The possibilities are endless!

Just remember that no note passing should take place during classes. Always remember that your notes should never be hurtful to others. And if you have an outdoor mailbox, beware of rain!

WOULD YOU RATHER?

There are no real rules for this one, and no winner, but it's a fun way to learn more about your friends!

One person asks a question that begins with "Would you rather..." and ends with two choices. The others pick one of the choices. This game can continue for minutes or hours, and the more outrageous the choices, the better!

Here are some examples to get you started:

Would you rather eat ranch salad dressing for breakfast, lunch, and dinner every day for the rest of your life...OR... wear the same pair of socks (without washing them) every day for the rest of your life?

Would you rather live in a mansion with no indoor bathrooms...OR... a tiny two-room apartment with an enormous built-in pool?

Would you rather smell like anchovies ...OR... eat anchovies as the only topping on your pizza every Friday night?

TURN-OFF-THE-TV NIGHT

Sometimes it's fun to kick back and watch TV. But other times it can be more fun to keep the TV off for the night. Every once in a while, try planning a Turn Off the TV Night for your friends.

To make the evening official, make invitations and distribute them to your friends one week before the big night. If your parents agree, tell your friends they can even bring their brother or sister. Look through your kitchen cupboards and plan a snack menu, and make sure to pick some activities for you and your friends to do together.

In addition to having fun with your friends, being nice to your sister is a good way to make you look good the next time you ask for a raise in your allowance!

LEND A HAND
SIMPLE PROJECTS TO BRIGHTEN SOMEONE'S DAY

Decorate-o-rama

We could all use some appreciation every now and then. Your friends are very special people, so when they do something extra special, you should let everyone know about it. And there's no better way to tell the world about your friend's accomplishment than to post it outside of her locker.

All you have to do is to get the okay from your teacher and then head into school early one morning. You can use posters, streamers, glitter, or anything that will tell the rest of the school about your friend's accomplishment, whether it's scoring the winning goal at yesterday's soccer game, getting the lead in the school play, or being voted class president. Even if she pretends to be embarrassed, your friend will LOVE the time and effort you put into this project.

As you know, hall decorations don't stay up forever. So if your BFF wants to keep her locker decorations looking nice, she may want to move them inside her locker!

Share a Smile

If people smiled more, the world would be a much happier place!

Collect five pieces of paper or note cards, decorate them, and write on each one: Thanks for the smile! You really made my day. Pass it on.

The next time someone does something nice for you, even as simple as opening the door, leave one of these note cards for her or him. Chances are that you will make that person's day, and hopefully she or he will pass along the message to someone else.

And you never know, maybe someone will give one of the note cards back to you! Smiles are contagious! One size fits all!

Thanks for the smile! You really made my day! :)

NOTABLE QUOTABLES: TALKING ABOUT FRIENDSHIP

Is your BFF feeling down? Try leaving her a note with one of these quotations about friendship!

A true friend is someone who makes something as boring as staring at a tissue box seem like fun.

—*Kate Hawley*

If all my friends were to jump off a bridge, I wouldn't jump with them, I'd be at the bottom to catch them. Everyone hears what you say. Friends listen to what you say. Best friends listen to what you don't say. We all take different paths in life, but no matter where we go, we take a little of each other everywhere.

—*Tim McGraw*

Peace. Love. Friendship. Chinese Broccoli in Garlic Sauce.

—*Brett Fletcher*

Strangers are just friends waiting to happen.

—*Unknown*

Have I told you lately how much I admire you?
Yes, you've always suspected this was the case,
and I'm here to confirm your suspicions. I don't
know...you're just pretty darn amazing. That's all.

—*Staci Shultz*

Dear George,
Remember, no man's a failure who has friends.
Thanks for the wings. Love, Clarence.

—*Clarence the Angel,* It's a Wonderful Life

PRINCESS POWER

Everyone likes a little special attention every now and then, so why not be royalty for the day? Your BFF is special, so treat her like a princess! When your friend least expects it, or when she

has had a rough week, make a plan with your group of friends to elect her Princess for the Day!

Make her a princess poster.

On the day you have chosen, tape it to her desk before school. When she first sits down that morning, she will be pleasantly surprised to find out what she has in store for her that day!

Treating someone like royalty can involve many different things. You don't need to bow down before your friend, but you could bring an extra dessert for her, let her in front of you in the lunch line, do whatever she wants to do during recess, give her your extra stick of gum, or let her use your fancy pen. And if you can schedule a sleepover the same night, let the princess choose the movies and the snacks!

The best part is that the princess now has the power to decide who will be the next Princess for the Day. This way, every one of your close friends can have a turn to be princess!

SHOE BOX SURPRISES

It's always fun to use your allowance to go to the mall or see a movie with your friends on the weekend. But for just one week a month, wouldn't it be nice to use your allowance in a different way? Especially if you still get to go shopping?!

Everyone likes getting presents, so why not use your money to create a care package for someone in a nursing home or hospital? To do this, you and your friends can save up a few dollars, then find an empty shoe box (preferably one

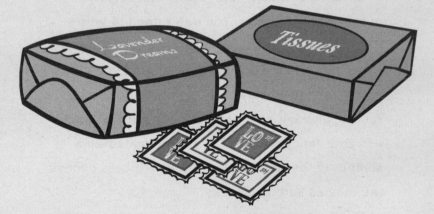

with a separate lid). If there aren't any in your closet, check the attic. Take your shoe box to the dollar store or a discount drugstore. Head to the section with the little travel samples, pick out a few (making sure they all fit in your shoe box), and go to the checkout line.

These are some things you can buy:

Tissues ★ Stationery ★ Stamps

Hand lotion ★ Body spray

Crossword puzzle books ★ Hard candy

Pens or pencils ★ Fancy soap

When you get home, wrap the shoe box with

pretty wrapping paper (or
even wrapping paper that
you make yourself) and then
wrap the shoe box lid sepa-
rately so the box can be used
for storage. Fill the box with

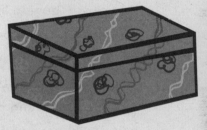

tissue paper and lay the presents inside. Place
the lid on top and tie it together with a brightly
colored ribbon (maybe a ribbon you have left
over from making your belt!). Make a card to
attach to the package.

Ask a parent or teacher to help you find a local
nursing home or hospital that will accept outside
gifts so you and your friends can deliver the Shoe
Box Surprises. You'll feel great about spending
your allowance this way, and you'll be making
someone else's day a little brighter. Caring
counts!

LOCKS OF LOVE

Don't you love to get your hair cut? How about getting your hair cut for free? And wouldn't it be great if doing something as easy as getting your hair cut could help someone else? With Locks of Love, it can!

Locks of Love is a nonprofit organization. They make wigs for kids who have medical problems that cause them to lose their hair. In fact, most of the wigs are made because girls just like you have donated their hair. You can help by simply having your hair cut!

Grab a ruler and measure the length of your hair. If you have your parents' permission and have 10 inches to cut off, you can help! Go to www.locksoflove.org to find a participating salon that will cut your hair for free! Make sure to have your hairstylist cut your hair while it is in a pony-tail or braid. Place the dry hair in a plastic bag, then in a padded mailing envelope to send to Locks of Love. Complete instructions and infor-mation are on the Web site.

Don't forget to take before and after pictures!

If your hair isn't long enough, let it grow! Set a goal to let your hair grow for the whole school year, and ask your friends if they'd like to join you.

NOTABLE QUOTABLES: FAMOUS THOUGHTS ABOUT FRIENDSHIP

The better part of one's life consists of his friendships. —*Abraham Lincoln*

Grief can take care of itself, but to get the full value of joy you must have somebody to divide it with. —*Mark Twain*

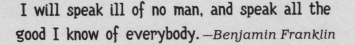

I will speak ill of no man, and speak all the good I know of everybody. —*Benjamin Franklin*

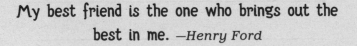

If you judge people, you have no time to love them. —*Mother Teresa*

My best friend is the one who brings out the best in me. —*Henry Ford*

NOTABLE QUOTABLES:

SOON-TO-BE-FAMOUS
THOUGHTS ABOUT FRIENDSHIP

My Thoughts About Friendship:

_____

_____

_____

_____

_____

_____

_____

_____

_____

_____

_____

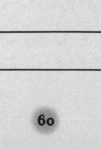

My BFF's Thoughts About Friendship:

_____

_____

_____

_____

_____

_____

_____

_____

_____

_____

_____

WORTH A THOUSAND WORDS

What's more fun—taking pictures or seeing how the pictures turn out?

Try taking pictures with black and white film. Buy a roll of black and white film (make sure you ask a salesperson for help, because there are lots of different kinds). Load it  into your camera and snap away ...but don't clue your friends in.

When your black and white film is developed, it will make even ordinary pictures seem professional and special.

You can tape the black and white pictures to red paper and frame them as gifts for your friends!

BRAIN POWER SOLUTIONS

Answers to pages 38-39:

1. Trick question! Survivors are still alive, so they aren't buried at all!

2. Did you place the dot above the letter instead of on it? Here's how it should look:

3. You are the bus driver, so the color of your eyes is the correct answer.

4. Girl power! The surgeon is Jason's mother.

Answers to page 44:

1. Three degrees below zero
2. Jack-in-the-box
3. Sun rising
4. Hole in one
5. Peace, Love and Understanding
6. Ring Around the Rosie

Answer to Page 45:

I hate to break it to you, but there actually is no answer to this one. The Mystery of the Missing Dollar is a problem without a solution. If you're upset because you spent a lot of time trying to figure it out, pass this along to someone else and watch her squirm!

CONCLUSION

If you are reading this, then you and your BFF have probably completed this book from front to back and from head to toe. And hopefully it has made you closer and more "JOINED AT THE HIP" than ever!

But if your BFF happens to live far away, don't worry. You may be too far away to be joined at the hip, but you'll always be JOINED BY THE HEART!